28 DAYS

Keys to Mastering Menstrual Madness and Mayhem

Taomi Ray

© March 2021, Dyersburg TN

<u>Table of Contents</u>

Introduction

The natural born female lives an existence that is both a blessing and a curse. Creating life is a very big deal but all the intricate details that go into that process create multiple scenarios and many years of frustration and down right confusion. The first opportunity to create life comes at a critical stage in a female's life, the onset of the menstrual cycle.This tabu topic is so serious that it need not remain a silent mystery plaguing the entire life of a woman.Lurking in the shadows of jokes and embarrassing outbursts. The menstrual cycle is a blessing because it is responsible for the creation of life but it is also a curse because it is the very culprit that can equally be responsible for systematically destroying a woman's entire quality of life.

Menstrual madness is a menace to society. From puberty all the way to menopause the female is attacked both physically and mentally and all this is happening internally on a rolling schedule (with a mind of its own). Constant and somewhat like clockwork, any woman at any given moment just might turn into a monster. Most women will silently agree, but only the bold and brave will openly state the facts. For all of those that are open to explore the possibilities of understanding one of the most complicated subjects known to man, this book is for you. This book was written to encourage you on your journey to self improvement in matters that are often seen as inappropriate conversation. Today we will bring this conversation to the masses and open the closet on what some say is the "curse of Eve".

Let us take a closer look at what we are actually dealing with and let us learn together how to deal with these issues in a better manner. Not with superstitious notions that leave us stuck in the past, but with reason and logic and information that will lead us into a better future where mankind can be seen and accepted as equal (and that means women too). Let us seek out the keys to mastering menstrual madness and mayhem.

<u>Chapter 1- Write It All Down</u>

I remember when I got my first diary. It was 1988. It was cute, it was pink and it had a lock and key. I thought the lock and key was everything at that time. It meant that no one would see this but me. I also liked the way the pages had shiny edges just like those on the pages of a KingJames Bible. In the 1980's I was a bible thumping church jumping bona fide "good girl". I was in middle school so that made me all of 12 years old. I thought I had it all figured out. I thought I knew how the world worked and all I wanted more than anything else was to go to heaven. I was so infatuated with the idea of going to heaven that I was fanatical about determining who would go to hell. Each church service I attended in the sectors of Baptist, C.O.G.I.C and Apostolic, indoctrinated me about ideas concerning what was right and what was wrong. In many cases those ideas morphed into discussing who was right and who was wrong. (I realized many years later who and what are NOT the same thing but at 12 it seemed like a good way to think). Sermons and bible studies revolved continually around the topics of who would be saved and who would bust hell wide open. Every colorful message on any given Sunday left me further questioning and contemplating. At 12 I had only 2 questions: 1- Was I going to heaven? 2- Why or why not? I often wrote down my thoughts.

The diary I received gave me a wide open space to contemplate and collect my thoughts in a private way. As a pre-teen I was an awkward girl. Tall, thin, big head, boofy hair, no boobs and no butt. I looked plain and average. As the 80's gave way to the early 1990's it seemed like I began to understand myself less and less. I had an undying curiosity about the world around me (the one I thought I knew all about at 12). I wanted to understand what it meant to be a woman. There were so many definitions of womanhood set before me, it was difficult to figure out what kind of woman I wanted to be.

I held on to the diary for many years. I often looked back to the pages of the 12 year old me when I got my first period at 14. Some would call me a late bloomer but nevertheless I was blooming all the way. The funny thing about the whole experience was that there seemed to be very little conversation about the matter when it happened. I expected more, I hoped for more, but instead I was sent to the bathroom with feminine products that I had never used and a feeling on the inside that never went away. The feeling was frustration. I was frustrated that I had soiled my underwear, I was frustrated about what it meant to now be " a woman" and I was very frustrated about the lack of conversation about the situation.

As the years progressed I found that many young women had a similar experience. Many girls have been thrust into the claws of womanhood with a pamphlet, a maxi pad and a prayer.

Writing in a diary or journaling on a regular basis has been proven by research. According to https://www.verywellmind.com " *It has been determined that those who keep a journal are more likely to be connected to their emotions and problem-solving skills. Keeping a journal has also been found to help a person relieve stress, let go of negativity, refocus on gratitude, and work through difficult emotions and circumstances.*" Writing it all down is a great way to begin the journey toward a better quality of life, it will start the process that will release you from the figurative chains that arrest every natural born female from 12-50. These chains were attached to our chromosomes at the time of conception, these chains are called hormones. Until you actively seek to understand the hormones behind the menstrual cycle in all of its splendor, you will never be able to trace them or track them. If you can't do that you are forced to live a life of unexpected upsets and unforgettable episodes of pure hormonal energy. These are the episodes that epic sagas are made of, these episodes create madness and mayhem in the life of what would be an ordinary woman on an ordinary day.

There are two primary hormones responsible for wreaking havoc and wrecking your life. The first hormone to trace and track is **estrogen**. She is really something! She just comes and goes as she pleases and leaves behind the bodies of all the lives she gets to ruin in her wake. According to www.MedicalNewsToday.com *"Estrogen is a hormone that plays various roles in the body. In females, it helps develop and* *maintain both the reproductive system and female characteristics, such as breasts and pubic hair. Estrogen contributes to cognitive health, bone health, the function of the cardiovascular system, and other essential bodily processes."* So yea this pretty much affects A LOT in the life of an ordinary woman. Tracking the rising and falling patterns of estrogen in your body is a must. There is more, estrogen is not alone, it has a whole crew of sidekicks!

"There are different types of estrogen:

Estrone
This type of estrogen is present in the body after menopause. It is a weaker form of estrogen and one that the body can convert to other forms of estrogen, as necessary.

Estradiol
Both males and females produce estradiol, and it is the most common type of estrogen in females during their reproductive years.

Too much estradiol may result in acne, loss of sex drive, osteoporosis, and depression. Very high levels can increase the risk of uterine and breast cancer. However, low levels can result in weight gain and cardiovascular disease. (seriously!!)

Estriol
Levels of estriol rise during pregnancy, as it helps the uterus grow and prepares the body for delivery. Estriol levels peak just before birth."

The second hormone to be on the lookout for is called **Progesterone**. *"Progesterone is the main progestational steroid hormone secreted by the female reproductive system. It is linked to the menstrual cycle, pregnancy, and development of an embryo...Progesterone travels in the blood to tissues where there are progesterone receptors. It attaches to the receptors to produce actions in the* *body...After puberty starts, the ovaries release a single egg each month. This process is called ovulation. The egg moves down the fallopian tube, and if it meets with sperm, it may be fertilized...If a woman does not ovulate, her ovaries do not produce progesterone. This is called an anovulatory cycle. Missed cycles often take place from the mid 30s onwards and become more frequent as menopause approaches...Progesterone levels drop consistently just before the menopause. This is thought to be the major cause of symptoms experienced around the menopause."*

Just these two hormones alone (including the sidekicks) seem to serve as the sheriff and deputy of the whole life of a woman. They are a hard nosed, hot headed and trigger happy group running around in our bodies and wreaking havoc on our lives! It may seem comical but for every person that has any connection to a female (and we all do) the reality is a lot harder to deal with and this topic is definitely not a joke.

This book was written with the sole purpose to help anyone who is struggling with the effects of all things menstrual (including menopause). Obviously women between the ages of 15-50 are the target audience. However, I would hope there would be some men brave enough to accept the challenge of understanding this life long mystery. Many husbands, boyfriends, brothers and bosses have to deal with an ongoing stream of mayhem all stemming from these hormones that think they rule the world. Today we will take the power back. Today we will get on track and find some answers and seek solutions.

<u>Chapter 2- Count It All Up</u>

In order to take charge of any situation you must first begin with documentation. Start counting stuff up. Actively review your diaries or journals, especially those that reveal symptomatic days and moments.

At one point I thought the only problem was with the thing called PMS (Premenstrual Syndrome). I thought that was supposed to happen before a period and that there would be no other issues except the actual flow. Then I found out for myself that there are multiple phases of the menstrual cycle and PMS is only a small sliver of the process. Menopause seems to work the same way, there are multiple stages of menopause that can take an additional 10-15 years to work through. I find it humorous that throughout history "female issues" have been thought of as just a myth, something women made up to make excuses to behave badly or get out of work or school. According to an article published by the Huffington Post: *"In an excerpt from the book Hot Flushes, Cold Science: A History Of The Modern Menopause, author Louise Foxcroft says the term "hysteria" was often used by doctors in describing their menopausal patients. (Gee, wonder where they got that idea??)*

The book gives accounts from the mid-1800s in England of doctors prescribing a pre-meal mixture of carbonated soda. Other remedies included a large belladonna plaster placed at the pit of the stomach and vaginal injections with a solution of acetate of lead. No wonder women were reduced to hysteria! Prescriptions ranged from opium and hydrochlorate of morphine to chloric ether and distilled water." It's crazy how we do things out of the lack of knowledge or the lack of interest. What we don't know becomes some mythological monster that we spend time conjuring up cures to get rid of. What we are not interested in is often the perspective of males who don't experience any of this and for those females who experience very mild symptoms. If it doesn't happen to you then you think everyone it IS happening to must be crazy. For the sake of proper documentation let us examine the phases of the menstrual cycle in their entirety.

According to www.WebMd.com "PMS is a group of changes that can affect you on many levels. They can be physical, emotional, or behavioral. The changes come 1 to 2 weeks before your period. PMS shows up in many different ways. Everything in this list could be a sign of PMS."

Physical signs
*Bloated tummy
*Cramps
*Tender breasts
*Hunger
*Headache
*Muscle aches

*Joint pain
*Swollen hands and feet
*Pimples
*Weight gain
*Constipation or diarrhea

<u>Emotional signs</u>
*Tense or anxious
*Depressed
*Crying
*Mood swings
*Can't sleep
*Don't want to be with people
*Feel overwhelmed or out of control
*Angry outbursts

<u>Behavioral signs</u>
*Forget things
*Loss of mental focus
*Tired

If you are as exhausted as I am just from looking at this list then let us take a moment and catch our breath (whoosa). Now that we see what PMS can look like, let's look at the other phases of the menstrual cycle (because it just keeps getting

better and better right).
According to
www.betterhealth.vic.gov " The
four phases of the menstrual cycle
are menstruation, the follicular
phase, ovulation and the luteal
phase." So great, you get the
luxury of spending two weeks out
of a four week month suffering
from PMS then you get to have 3
more excruciating phases that make
life even more adventurous. Let's
keep counting and see how long
each phase lasts.

Health experts say that the first
day of the typical "28" day cycle
begins with the shedding of blood
(What a way to start out the
month). <u>Menstruation</u> is the
elimination of the thickened
lining of the uterus (endometrium)
from the body through the vagina.
Menstrual fluid contains blood,
cells from the lining of the
uterus (endometrial cells) and
mucus. The average length of a
period is between <u>three days and
one week</u>. So did you get that,
another week just gone down the

drain because you are actually shedding blood. Two weeks of PMS, one week of bloodshed, and we are still not done counting.

The next phase is the <u>follicular</u> phase, it starts on the first day of menstruation and ends with ovulation. Prompted by the hypothalamus, the pituitary gland releases follicle stimulating hormone (FSH). This hormone stimulates the ovary to produce around five to 20 follicles (tiny nodules or cysts), which bead on the surface. Each follicle houses an immature egg. Usually, only one follicle will mature into an egg, while the others die. This can occur <u>around day 10 </u>of a 28-day cycle. The growth of the follicles stimulates the lining of the uterus to thicken in preparation for possible pregnancy. There is good news about this phase because research shows that usually during this time period, your estrogen and testosterone levels begin to build again. Increased hormonal activity means you may have a heightened sense of smell, along with clearer thinking and better coordination. Many women, in fact, report <u>feeling their best</u> at this time of the month — physically and mentally. "You'd be likely to do better with a final exam if you're in school, or a presentation if you're at work," Doctors say. You may also experience an increase in sex drive during this phase. So this might be the only winner in the hand, it would be wise to figure out when this phase begins in your life and use it to your advantage. Write it down and count down your days every month.

Just when you feel like a winner and not a loser, here comes probably the most important phase, <u>ovulation</u>. This is the phase where you can get pregnant. During the ovulation phase, Luteinizing hormone (LH) surges from the pituitary gland, triggering ovulation about 24 to 36 hours later. Your ovary will then release a mature egg that travels towards the uterus in search of a sperm. According to Heathline, you'll begin to ovulate right in the middle of your menstrual cycle, which is <u>around day 14</u> if you have a 28-day cycle. It lasts about 24 hours, and if the egg isn't fertilized it will dissolve. This phase has a good and bad side. According to Hal Danzier, M.D., reproductive endocrinologist and cofounder of Southern California Reproductive Center, estrogen and testosterone rise to peak levels, boosting the effects of the follicular phase. *"Women feel more energy, more sex drive, and often they notice more cervical mucus," Dr. Danzier explains. "The chemistry of your body is preparing for reproduction, so it makes sense that chemically you start feeling more inclined to have sex."* In other words you feel really sexy but you are also experiencing a huge amount of discharge (cervical mucus). Well that's just great! How can you really feel sexy when you have a bunch of gunk in your underwear? That just might make you irritated or annoyed and we know that doesn't help the situation one bit. That's not even the end of it, according to www.healthline.com *"Most women experience a range of different types of discharge throughout their menstrual cycle. You may produce around a teaspoon of thick or thin, odorless mucus each day, and the color can change from white to clear to brown. You might not realize it, but what you see isn't totally random. The different colors and textures have to do with your hormones and what's going on inside your body at the time. There are other downsides, also. "Right around ovulation is the time when many women experience acne breakouts, or single pimples, usually recurring in the same area," Dr. Danzier says. Additionally, you can expect breast tenderness, weight gain, headaches, and water retention. The fleeting moment of feeling sexy is often overshadowed by the gunk in the underwear, acne and breast tenderness! All of* these things are actually going on in the life of any ordinary woman on any given day and we wonder why some women seem so mad. We also wonder why some men feel so deprived. Once again we are reminded of the pesky hormones that started all this mess in the first place. As funny as it may sound I hope you are still keeping up with the count. So as of now, we have a 2 week PMS, a 1 week shedding of blood phase, a 2 day ovulation moment (that is literally a miniature moment)and now we get to see discharges of varying colors and textures (and we might see discharge everyday). Just when you might think it is actually over and you can return to being a normal human being, guess what...another phase.

The last phase of the menstrual cycle is the _luteal phase_. According to www.VeryWell.com *"it begins after ovulation, post-_day 14_, and _continues until the first day of your period_. In this phase, hormones thicken and ripen the uterus to get it ready for pregnancy. During this post-ovulation phase, many women feel hot. "Increased progesterone acts on the temperature-regulating area in the brain. It can rise about four-tenths of a degree in this phase, from 98.6 to about 99 degrees. Increased progesterone also relaxes the smooth muscle of the uterus as well as your gallbladder, sphincter and intestines. That means you may look and feel more bloated."* Did you notice that this phase ends right at the beginning so the whole thing can start all over again. Do we get a break or a timeout or an intervention or something? Nope, this is just the way it is. This is the sad story of the 28 days of menstrual madness and mayhem! It is an ongoing epic saga that can cause you to feel overwhelmed, anxious and angry. Were you counting with me? Did you notice that there are only 30-31 days in a whole month and look at what happens over the course of 28 of those days. It is enough to make you put your head down and throw your hands up. Try not to feel hopeless. Science has come a long way since the days when doctors just called this whole thing hysteria. More and more research is out in the world and it is up to each individual to get the information, count up the days, map out a plan and do the work.

<u>Chapter 3-Prepare A Plan</u>

A positive thought before mapping out a good plan.

2 Corinthians 4:8-18 (King James Version)

8 We are troubled on every side, yet not distressed; we are perplexed, but not in despair;

9 Persecuted, but not forsaken; cast down, but not destroyed;

10 Always bearing about in the body the dying of the Lord Jesus, that the life also of Jesus might be made manifest in our body.

11 For we which live are always delivered unto death for Jesus' sake, that the life also of Jesus might be made manifest in our mortal flesh.

12 So then death worketh in us, but life in you.

13 *We having the same spirit of faith, according as it is written, I believed, and therefore have I spoken; we also believe, and therefore speak;*

14 *Knowing that he which raised up the Lord Jesus shall raise up us also by Jesus, and shall present us with you.*

15 *For all things are for your sakes, that the abundant grace might through the thanksgiving of many redound to the glory of God.*

16 *For which cause we faint not; but though our outward man perish, yet the inward man is renewed day by day.*

17 *For our light affliction, which is but for a moment, worketh for us a far more exceeding and eternal weight of glory;*

18 *While we look not at the things which are seen, but at the things which are not seen: for the things*

which are seen are temporal; but the things which are not seen are eternal."

With all that we have discussed in this book it may seem that God must be "out to get us". It may very well appear that what females have to endure is totally unbearable and by far unreasonable. Fortunately, we can say this in all honesty, what doesn't kill you WILL make you stronger! We must believe in something or all is lost. We must hope for something or we will be lost. Try to take this information and strategically change your life. If you are a woman who has been living life on a day by day basis and letting things just happen as they happen, this might be a good time to sit down and strategize your next 28 days.

Get a calendar, start with the first day of your last period and count all the way until the start of the next period. This is where you must begin. You must see each phase as they occur. If you fail to recognize the onset of certain phases you will be blindsided every time. Month after month you will find yourself having angry outbursts, moments of depression and fits of anxiety. The funny thing is you might not even notice it, you might just blame it on everyone else around you. You might even get upset at the audacity of someone to blame the menstrual cycle for the actions of rational human beings. It seems like an insult, but let me let you in on a secret...it is true! The hormones at play are responsible for the behaviors, the emotions, the feelings,the acne, the weight gain etc. You might ask, how can we go to war with hormones in our bodies? We can't see, feel, hear or touch these hormones, so how are we supposed to defeat them? How are we supposed to keep them from running our whole lives for almost the whole month every month of the year. The answer is beat them at their own game. We are going to dig into some resources and strategies. We are also going to find ways to reward ourselves when we get things right. So let us look up. Let us get ready to take life back. These hormones will no longer run you or ruin you when you can see them coming and when you can call them by their names! Get your calendar and let's get ready to rumble!

<u>Chapter 4-Resources and Rewards</u>

We will start and end this chapter with information from experts. This chapter will discuss how to feel and be your best during each phase.

Phase 1- The menstrual Flow
If you're extra tired during your period, take it easy and rest more than you usually do. Erika Schwartz, M.D., an internist and author of The Hormone Solution, recommends using heating pads for aches and discomfort as well as low doses of Advil, Aleve, or Tylenol with codeine if pain is persistent. And avoid caffeine, she says, as it constricts blood vessels and increases tension.

Phase 2- The Follicular Phase
According to Lauri Grossman, chair of the Department of Medicine and Humanistic Studies at the American Medical College of Homeopathy,"Women also experience positive sensations such as relief, release, euphoria, new

beginning, invigoration, connection with nature, creative energy, exhilaration, increased sex drive and more intense orgasms." Pinpoint this phase on your calendar for sure! Consider brainstorming or problem-solving during this phase, as well as doing things that capitalize on your creative energy. Be social and go out with friends. This would be the best time for family movie nights, date night with the bae or work related social activities.

Phase 3- Ovulation
As this phase is a period of "renewal of sexual relationships," you can take the time to try to reconnect with your lover, says Inga Zilberstein, MD, a New York City-based OB/GYN. No matter what stage of life you're in, there's a lot you can do to heat things up in the bedroom. Since this is also the time of increased discharge, here is more info maintaining a healthy vagina. (source https://www.healthywomen.org/)

Keep the vagina clean and dry

Cotton is breathable, making it an ideal fabric selection for underwear. It can down on moisture as it keeps your skin cool and dry. With breathable fabrics like cotton, you have a reduced risk of bacterial growth and infections. On the flip side, fabrics like satin retain moisture. That reduces airflow, creating irritation and friction. And that encourages yeast and bacteria growth, which can lead to infections. You should also change out of sweaty workout clothing and wet swimsuits to help prevent infections.

Don't douche

Your vagina knows how to take care of itself. It self-cleans and naturally produces some discharge that helps get rid of germs and bacteria from your body. So, douching or using harsh cleaners or soaps can disrupt your natural pH balance and can irritate your vagina and wash away good bacteria. Plus, douching will only mask the smell—not cure what's going on. For example, if your vagina smells like something rotting (such as rotten fish), you may have bacterial vaginosis, a common vaginal infection. Stick with warm water and mild soap on the vulva.

Eat right
Maintaining a healthy diet can do your body and your vagina good. Foods like yogurt with live cultures contain good-for-you bacteria that help promote vaginal health. If you're prone to urinary tract infections, research in Archives of Internal Medicine suggests it may be helpful to take a cranberry supplement daily.

Use fresh towels
Wash and replace towels and washcloths after you use them. Reusing towels isn't wise because bacteria can cling to these surfaces. And that potentially puts you at risk for an infection.

Practice safe sex

The Centers for Disease Control & Prevention says that consistent and correct use of latex condoms reduces the risk of any sexually transmitted diseases that are transmitted by genital fluids such as gonorrhea, chlamydia and trichomoniasis. However, condoms provide less protection against STDs spread through skin-to-skin contact like genital warts, genital herpes and syphilis, says the U.S. Food and Drug Administration.

When condoms don't protect against STDs, it's usually because they're being used inconsistently or incorrectly, not because they failed. For example, some people use a condom just during ejaculation or sometimes have intercourse without a condom, you should put a condom on sex toys because certain infections can be transmitted on them. Clean toys with soap and water if the product allows.

Stay clean

It sounds simple but it's important to wipe from front to back until the toilet paper shows no residue. That will help prevent bacteria from getting into the vagina. Change sanitary pads and tampons regularly during your period. If you're wearing panty liners, change them frequently. However, if you wear them all the time, you may have some irritation.

Phase 4-The Luteal Phase

Avoid salty foods, which can contribute to water retention and more bloat. Also try to avoid sugar and processed foods whenever possible, health experts say, "Roller-coastering your blood sugar will only exacerbate the chemical reaction of your hormones,". Plus, try not to blow off the gym — even if you really don't feel up to it. "Forty five minutes of walking, swimming or any mild to moderate exercise has a positive effect on many women,".

For some women, though, PMS can bring on extreme mood swings. You'll want to talk to your doctor about an action plan if you think you may be experiencing extreme behavior.

Now that you know what you know, reward yourself for taking the time to learn. You could have been doing anything else with your day but instead you were reading this book gaining valuable insight that will help you maintain a better quality of life. A reward is anything that makes you feel happy about an accomplishment. Let your rewards be healthy and safe. You might not have much money or you might have a great deal of money. A reward is not about how much it costs, it is about a positive reinforcement for wanted behaviors. Each month you document that you kept your cool and did not lose your temper. Give yourself a reward. Each month that you added water or vitamins to your skin or hair care regimen, you should get a reward. Don't

wait for anyone else to give you
this reward, do it for yourself.
If you like flowers, order some
and have them sent to your job. If
you like nice restaurants, find
one nearby and take a night out
either with friends, spouse or
even solo. If you are a reader,
dive into a new book that will
have you turning pages and into a
world of your own. Whatever makes
you smile and lights you up, use
that as a reward. Never give up on
yourself even if you have a bad
month (they will still happen).
The keys to mastering menstrual
madness include patience,
persistence and perseverance. We
all have one life to live and we
have to live it to the fullest. We
can't afford to sit by and watch
months go down the drain with bad
memories and even worse
consequences for bad behavior.
Blaming the hormones will not work
at the job. The workplace is where
you test your new skill set. Try
out a new breathing technique when
you get frustrated. Pointing out
the fact that you are in a certain

phase of your menstrual cycle may not be a good idea when your significant other wants to be romantic and does not understand you have tender breasts. Share the info you have but find a happy medium that will keep you both satisfied. We wreak havoc in our lives when we feel out of control. So what is the answer? Get in control. Write down all the negative episodes. Keep up with your phases with a calendar or use your cell phone calendar. Most importantly don't forget to reward yourself for doing the right thing the right way. Where there is a will there IS a way. You can live a normal life in spite of the various hormones attacking your body and mind at all times. You are still a WINNER! You were born for this so let's do it!

Chapter 5- Products To Try and Books To Read

Books

PERIOD POWER: A MANIFESTO FOR THE MENSTRUAL MOVEMENT BY NADYA OKAMOTO, ILLUSTRATED BY REBECCA ELFAST

Give this book to every menstruator in the world! Nadya opens with her own story of her first period, because the goal of the book is to dispel all discomfort surrounding menstruation, and she CRUSHES it. She also is intentional about removing gender from menstruation: let's say people who menstruate, not women. Menstrual products, not "feminine hygiene products." This is a perfect book for young people who menstruate, and really, also young people who don't menstruate. Period Power is an accessible book chock full o' information about the culture, history, and privilege that goes along with this most basic of bodily functions.

PERIODS GONE PUBLIC: TAKING A STAND FOR MENSTRUAL EQUITY BY JENNIFER WEISS-WOLF

Periods aren't secret little taboos anymore. They're a big, loud political issue, and Jennifer Weiss-Wolf breaks it down for us, with historical and cultural context across the world, along with tons of activism ideas to get your blood pumping. Periods Gone Public is a must-read.

PERIOD: TWELVE VOICES TELL THE BLOODY TRUTH BY KATE FARRELL

This right here is a gorgeously designed collection of essays about menstruation. Every topic—and maybe even topics you wouldn't think of—are covered here. Madame Gandhi writes about free bleeding while running the London Marathon. Wiley Reading writes about being a trans man with a period. Emma Straub writes about living with a horrendously painful period without questioning it for far too long.

Products

AZO Happy Cycle™ is specially formulated with naturally sourced ingredients like Chaste Tree Berry Extract—derived from a plant that has been used by women for thousands of years to support hormonal health.*
Plus Ashwagandha—an Ayurvedic herb that provides mood support and reduces stress to help you stay happy and upbeat, anytime of the month*.
When taken daily, AZO Happy CycleTM helps support:
Positive Mood*
Daily Stress Relief*
Cramping & Bloating Relief*
A Regular & Consistent Cycle*
Plus it helps boost & sustain energy.*
https://www.azoproducts.com/products/hormonal-health/azo-happy-cycle

Price
$22.00

MOODY BIRD®

Helps manage symptoms of PMS*
This formula uses a potent herbal blend to support healthy hormone balance + ease symptoms of PMS.
What it does
Reduces severity of PMS symptoms including cramps, mood swings + irritability.Maintains healthy hormone balance.

How it works

Chaste berry is linked to progesterone production, supporting balanced hormones for reduced PMS symptoms
Dong quai root helps balance estrogen levels + replenish blood flow to help relieve cramps and provide a calming effect

60 vegan capsules · 30 days

https://www.humnutrition.com/product/19/moody-bird

Price
$26.00

Herbalogic Peacekeeper Drops
Peacekeeper combines powerful botanical extracts long used by traditional healers to restore balance and flatten the emotional peaks and valleys that often coincide with monthly periods.*

https://www.herbalogic.com/collections/

Price
$28.95

<u>Conclusion</u>

Thank you for taking the time to read this book. I hope the pages have inspired you to continue on your journey of self improvement. Mastering anything in life takes time, time, and more time. None of us will get it all right all the time. It is my hope that you will live a full life and experience all that the universe has to offer in a positive manner.

www.ingramcontent.com/pod-product-compliance
Lightning Source LLC
Chambersburg PA
CBHW060945130726
48001CB00003B/1069